From Darkness To Light

DONNA THORPE

WESTBOW®
PRESS
A DIVISION OF THOMAS NELSON
& ZONDERVAN

WestBow Press books may be ordered through booksellers or by contacting:

WestBow Press
A Division of Thomas Nelson & Zondervan
1663 Liberty Drive
Bloomington, IN 47403
www.westbowpress.com
1 (866) 928-1240

ISBN: 978-1-4908-3637-9 (sc)
ISBN: 978-1-4908-3636-2 (e)

Library of Congress Control Number: 2014908178

Printed in the United States of America.

WestBow Press rev. date: 05/15/2014

Contents

Acknowledgments...vii

No Greater Love 1
Your Ultimate Love 3
Unified in His Love 5
A Child of God...9
Thank You, Lord..11
He Is the Only Way 13
Praises Unending 15
Walk with Me...17
My Comfort Prayer...19
Daily Prayer 21
Our Savior Leads Us 23
Look unto Me..25
Our Forever Friend...27
Women Uniting in Grace 29
Spiritual Yearning..31
Redeemer 33
My Guide...35
God Brought Me Through 37
The Sun Always Shines..39
Bless Our Soldiers 41
Hands To Heaven 43
Sing Me into Heaven 45
No Good-Bye...47
Seek Me 49
Never Fear 51
God Save Our Nation 53

An Angel in Our Midst...55

Our Sister, Ivy..57

Suddenly Departed..59

Eternity Awaits 61

Forgiveness...63

From Darkness to Light 65

Acknowledgments

First and foremost, I would like to thank God for His inspiration of these writings. Since I was old enough to write, He has always guided my hand. I would also like to thank my dear family, and my brothers and sisters in Christ for their encouragement and support throughout this entire journey. A very special "thank-you" goes out to my dear sister in Christ, Frieda Halverson, for her incredible decorating on the Scripture illustration pages. Frieda has been my special and tireless companion during this wonderfully exciting time. I would also like to thank my wonderful husband, Paul. He has been my "angel," right by my side all through my incredible day-to-day walk with God. The cover of this book was specially designed by my brother in Christ, Kerry Denson. Brother Denson is not only an exquisite designer, he is also the minister at our church.

But above all things put on love,

which is the bond of perfection.

Colossians 3:14 (NKJV)

No Greater Love

No greater love has ever been shown,
Than the one our Savior gave for us alone.
He came to this earth to set us all free;
His sacrifice bought us our victory.

Jesus is with us each moment we live;
We must follow His Word to be saved.
Our lives should be beacons of light,
As examples of what is truly right.

Show the world that you belong to Him,
And, do your best to bring others to His side.
When following His pathway, others will see,
You guide them to be saved and free.

Your Ultimate Love

My dreams have been many;
My desires are few.
All that I do in my life,
I dedicate to You.

I yearn for Your love;
I bathe in its light.
I feel safe every day,
Into the darkest night.

You guide me to goodness;
I try to do right.
Even in disappointment,
You still give me might.

I strive for success,
Always keeping You near.
I give thanks for Your blessings,
Every day of the year.

Unified in His Love

Let us not dwell on
Separation and diversity.
Rather, come together in
Unification and solidarity.

All of us in this world,
Are children of God.
The love we share in our hearts,
Is derived from this divine blessing.

As children, we are innocent,
Unaware of hostility and cruelty,
In the world around us.

As we grow, our lives are affected
By school, family, and friends.
If we remain as "children,"
We will find favor with God.

Please remember that we all,
Must serve Him diligently.
God's love is colorless;
So should ours be for one another.

With each passing day, God shows us rainbows.
He blesses us with people in our lives;
They come in many colors, always blending perfectly,
So we may see them through His eyes.

God's perfect landscape each morning we see;
The people all around us, help complete the scene.
He allows us to see His image, in each and every face.
His wisdom reveals this to us; instead of a color scheme.

And we know that all things work

together for good to those who love God,

to those who are the called according to

His purpose.

Romans 8: 28 (NKJV)

A Child of God

I am a child of God,
Though humbly I say;
"I need my precious Jesus
To guide me through each day."

Even when I stumble,
And sometimes when I fall,
I know I have my Savior,
To help me through it all.

Without the hand of Jesus,
To help me find my way,
I know the pitfalls of this world,
Would all but wash me away.

So, my dear sisters and brothers,
In Christ we must unite.
To stand for our Christian faith,
And show this world what is right.

Please do not get discouraged,
Even when you feel blue,
Just trust Him with your life.
He will always comfort you.

Thank You, Lord

As Your humble servant,
I know that mere words
Cannot praise You to the heights,
That You deserve.

My prayers of earthly requests,
Are always in Your hands.
I must have faith,
That You alone can understand.

Thank you, Jesus, for hearing all my prayers,
Whether tearful or joyful.
I know You are always there.
Your miracles never go unnoticed.

He Is the Only Way

The only way is through Jesus;
He is the Light and the Way.
Our lives cannot go forward,
Without Him guiding us each day.

Praise Him in the morning,
And all day as we work or play.
When day is done and evening comes,
Praise Him as in slumber we lay.

On those days when rain falls down,
And clouds surround our hearts,
We need His precious love so near,
To calm our fears before they start.

Oh precious Savior Jesus, we love You,
And we praise You in everything we do.
Please help us to worship You and pray
For strength so we may follow You.

Thank you, Jesus, for going to the cross.
Without Your supreme sacrifice,
Our lives would surely be lost.
You are the only Way.

And now abide faith, hope, love,

these three; but the greatest of these is love.

1 Corinthians 13:13 (NKJV)

Praises Unending

Praise Him in the morning;
Praise Him all the time.
God is worthy always.
Praise Him, for His will is mine.

Unending songs and praises ring
From here upon the earth
To our sovereign King.
Praise Him with all we have.

With voices lifted high,
We testify to His might--.
From the moment we awaken,
Till deep within the night.

This is how He should be praised:
No holding back our spirits,
No time to walk away,
Praise Him in the highest always.

Praises in the morning,
Praises in the night.
The God of all creation,
Is precious in our sight.

I praise Him for His mercy,
I praise Him for His grace.
I praise Him because He loves me;
In spite of my mistakes.

I praise Him for every breath I take,
And, loving people to share my life.
I praise Him for a husband who is a humble servant;
And, a teacher, who has made me proud to be his wife.

God gave us His Son, so we could be saved;
Praise Him for that blessing of eternal life.
Praise Him without ceasing, He is worthy always.
Praise Him with all you do throughout your life.

Walk with Me

Walk with me, oh Savior mine,
And share with me Thy light divine.
For in my hours of peaceful rest,
You show me how my life is blessed.

Sweet Jesus, You light my way,
And guide me through each day.
At night, I pray that each new day,
I may follow Thee along life's way.

While on this earth, I look to Thee
To hold my hand and comfort me.
Though temptation tries to bother me,
With every breath, I will trust in Thee.

Walk with me, oh Savior mine,
And stay with me throughout all time.
Only You can guide me to eternal rest.
At the end, I will be heaven blessed.

My Comfort Prayer

When my heart is all broken
And I feel You are not there,
Whom shall I turn to
In my time of despair?

For I breathe not without You,
And cannot survive--.
Without Your sweet love,
I am no longer alive.

I gaze up to heaven,
Tears running down my face,
I pray Your forgiveness,
My sins will erase.

The way less traveled is
Sometimes hard to bear,
That is when I will feel You,
And know that You are there.

Daily Prayer

As you work
And as you play,
Please don't forget
To stop and pray.

God guides our thoughts;
He gives us His grace.
Remember to thank Him,
And praise His sweet name.

When days seem long,
And nothing is clear,
Pray for His wisdom,
He will always be near.

 And now abide faith, hope, love,

these three; but the greatest of these is love.

1 Corinthians 13:13 (NKJV)

Our Savior Leads Us

Tears of joy, tears of pain,
No fear of hurting,
No sad farewells--,
He will make us new again.

In doubt, we trust Him;
He always prevails,
In faith, we follow,
His Word never fails.

Walk in the light,
Though narrow the path.
Follow His steady footsteps;
He leads us to do right.

His love is unending;
This is why we survive.
Continue to share Him
Every day of your life.

Look unto Me

When times are dreary and full of woe,
It may seem that we have nowhere to go.
Look to our Savior; His will is divine.
Jesus directs us down the straight and narrow line.
His yearning is for us to join Him someday,
When all of our burdens have been lifted away.
While others may cause us such sorrow and pain,
We may think we will never be happy again.
Just look to our Savior, and remember His way.
Love one another, and rejoice in each day.

Our Forever Friend

There is no friend like Jesus;
He is steady to the end.
He is our Rock.
He is our hope.

Where on earth could we find,
Such a loyal friend?
In joy and in sorrow,
His love will see us through.

From our first breaths to our last,
We can depend on His strength.
Jesus, precious Savior,
Guide me to Your side.

When troubles have surrounded me,
I never had to worry, because I always knew;
That Jesus was there walking by my side.
In every situation, He has brought me through.

If not for Jesus, I would not be here today.
He healed me from breast cancer;
And, He guided me all the way.
There is no friend like Jesus, to show you the way.

Women Uniting in Grace

God gave women hearts of tenderness and mercy.
When we gather together in strength and compassion,
We serve Him with the passion He instilled in our souls.
Never holding back, always willing to do above and
beyond.
Together, we draw inspiration from one another to
prevail.
Our Savior is always by our side; He holds our
hands as we
Walk together with Him along the way He leads us.
Each and every breath we take, we give our very lives to
Take care of everyone God has placed in our paths.
Our spirits burn with the love straight from the
heart of God!

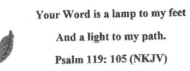

Your Word is a lamp to my feet

And a light to my path.

Psalm 119: 105 (NKJV)

Spiritual Yearning

If material possessions do not
Quench your desire,
Maybe Jesus is the only
One you should admire.

You may live in a mansion
High upon a hill.
But Jesus promises us a place,
If we do our Father's will.

By worldly things, we must
Not be led astray.
Jesus is the one true Light,
To help us find our way.

In my life, I have had friends lead me astray,
They turned out not to be true friends.
There have been times, I wanted material things,
Then, I realized, that Jesus was all I need.

The cars and boats and "toys" of life,
Have sometimes gotten in my way;
Which caused me nothing but daily strife.
Now, my focus is Jesus, He guides me every day.

Redeemer

Oh blessed night of His birth,
So all would know what life is worth--.
He came into this world so cold,
To give us love to have and hold.

He set a path for us to follow,
To keep our souls from becoming hollow.
He wandered this earth without riches or gain,
To show us His wisdom, and free us from pain.

His light of love shines forever bright,
From break of day to deep in the night.
We feel His love surround us,
With each and every breath we take.

And when our time on earth is done,
His mercy and grace will guide us home.
When we see Jesus, He will hold us dear,
He will welcome us to heaven, never more to fear.

My Guide

Take my hand, for I want to
Walk through life with You.
You are the only One I need,
To tell my troubles to.

I will follow Your love,
For the rest of my life--.
To try to love as You do,
Even through anger and strife.

You are always with me,
No matter where I go.
When everyone else is gone,
I know I can turn to You.

Rejoice in the Lord always.

Again I will say, rejoice!

Philippians 4: 4 (NKJV)

God Brought Me Through

You brought me through breast cancer.
You won for me the fight.
When others doubted your presence,
You showed to them Your might.

Through painful, scary surgery,
And radiation twenty-eight times,
A staph infection after it all,
And back into surgery again--.

You brought me out of death,
Stage zero to proclaim.
I thank you with every breath, my God,
And, forever praise Your name!

The Sun Always Shines

The sun always shines in my heart,
Though it may rain all around me,
I am no longer sad and alone.
My Savior fills my life with joy.

The warmth of His love grows each minute,
I feel the tranquility and calm every day.
The light of His love shines through.
Without His inspiration, I am numb.

Look at all the wonders around us;
They were made for us to enjoy.
Even when we do not understand,
He guides our eternal paths.

The sun always shines in my heart;
No clouds or gloom hide the warmth.
While going through my daily chores,
I thank Him for the blessings in my life.

My Savior is always by my side,
Through good and bad, He remains.
I am so blessed because of His grace.
The sun always shines in my heart.

Bless Our Soldiers

God bless our brave soldiers,
Each and every one.
Their fearless fight for freedom,
Continues from dawn to setting sun.

Some have returned to us
With wounds that cannot heal.
Some sacrificed all to make us
Know that their love was truly real.

Soldiers so courageous and true,
Daily defend the red, white, and blue.
Never forget to thank them each day.
They proudly stand for the American way.

God bless America!

Let all that you do be done with love.

1 Corinthians 16: 14 (NKJV)

Hands To Heaven

With our hands raised to heaven,
We glorify Thee--.
Songs full of praise,
And prayers on bended knee.

Our voices raised in song,
All hearts and souls rejoice.
We continue to worship Thee,
With a strong, resounding voice.

We reach our hands up high,
To let You know our love is true.
We live to worship You, Jesus,
In everything we do.

Sweet Jesus, Your love is our strength.
Walk with us through all our days.
Please hold us when we stumble,
And guide us in Your merciful ways.

Our hands raise toward heaven,
To praise and glorify Thee.
Every day in every way,
We live to worship Thee!

Sing Me into Heaven

Sing me into heaven,
As I leave this lonely world.
May voices rise in harmony,
To praise our Savior's name.

Please blend those voices sweetly,
To harmonize those tunes.
Sweet Jesus, we proclaim
This life's precious victory.

So, raise your voices to Him,
As you sing to me good-bye.
God loves to hear us singing,
Each note He hears on high.

Sing me into heaven,
Till we sing together again--.
When we all meet Jesus,
And forever sing with Him.

No Good-Bye

As you travel onward
Through life's ever-changing way,
May joy surround your journey,
As you walk from day to day.

Whenever clouds appear
And your horizon is not clear,
Remember those who love you,
Always keep you near.

So, never forget the treasure
You have brought to all our lives.
We will not say good-bye,
Though you may see sadness in our eyes.

"Farewell for now", is all we wish to say.
You will remain in our hearts.
Just think of us fondly and smile,
Know that you will see us in just a little while.

And you will seek Me and find Me,

when you search for Me with all your heart.

Jeremiah 29: 13 (NKJV)

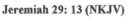

Seek Me

Seek Me when times turn bad.
Thank Me for all that you have.
Seek Me when you cannot see the light.
Seek Me through the darkest night.
Thank Me when the way grows clear.
Praise Me when I calm your fear.
Seek Me always in faces you see;
Know that you are looking at Me.
Seek Me when the end draws near.
Praise Me for always being here.

Never Fear

Never fear, for I am here--,
Every day, every hour,
Close enough to whisper in your ear.
My love creates this power.

Never fear; I will be near,
Even when you don't want Me,
I will dry all of your tears.
My life I gave for you.

Trust in Me, and you will soar;
The mountains you can climb.
Never fear, I will hold you near,
Until we are together in eternity.

God Save Our Nation

Thy Word be heard;
Thy Will be done.
Let Thy children speak,
And, not be silenced.

May our nation
Be blessed again--.
Return to His ways,
Giving praise unto Him.

For we know that without Thee,
We are led astray.
Let not the will of the wicked,
Become our daily bread.

Deliver us from sin and doubt;
Your faithful servants cry out for mercy.
Guide us through the dreadful darkness,
Terrorism has threatened on our soil.

Today and always, we know,
That You are with us.
Oh, God, have mercy on our nation,
And, our individual souls, we pray.

Blessed are the pure in heart,

For they shall see God.

Matthew 5: 8 (NKJV)

An Angel in Our Midst

She walked softly on this earth,
For only a little while--.
Long enough to be a treasured:
Daughter, mother, and endearing friend.

Although she has been called away,
She is at home in our hearts--.
Her sweet, giving ways remembered,
By all who knew her name.

God gave us this angel
To dwell in our midst.
She touched all of us,
Down to our very souls.

Her inspiration will live on,
In our day-to-day lives,
Knowing she is waiting for us
At the end of our journeys.

She had a smile that warmed us,
From the moment she saw your face.
She served your meal with pleasure,
In her sweet, kind way with grace..

This sweet angel has gone,
From our reach for now.
Some sweet day, we will
See her again in heaven.

Our Sister, Ivy

Sometimes God brings us "angels"
To lightly tread on our hearts.
A woman of faith who has inspired many,
Has touched our very souls with her loving spirit.
Her small stature did not describe her giant
Influence on the lives of everyone she knew.
God gave her the strength and grace to know
His Word and apply it to the way she lived.
A true servant of God in everything she did,
She ran the church kitchen with swift and mighty
precision.
The wisdom of her years was shared with those of us
Who were blessed enough to spend time with her.
God blessed each and every one of us, by allowing us
To enjoy the treasure of having Sister Ivy in our lives.
We know that she is resting until the day when we all
Will join her in heaven, with Jesus, our Lord.

Suddenly Departed

When loved ones are gone
In the blink of an eye,
Remember, He is with you,
To help you say good-bye.

When you are paralyzed with grief,
And, you feel like you are all alone.
Never lose hope in your Savior,
He will give your aching soul relief.

Never fear; He is always near--.
Close enough to catch your tears.
Cling to Him with all of your heart.
He will help you to make a new start.

But you are a chosen generation,

a royal priesthood, a holy nation,

His own special people,

that you may proclaim the praises of Him

who called you out of darkness

into His marvelous light.

1 Peter 2: 9 (NKJV)

Eternity Awaits

When the weight of this world
Seems impossible to bear,
Remember our sweet Savior,
Whose love is everywhere.

Pray often; show others your light,
Remember His great promise.
We will see His precious face,
In the land where there is no night.

When this world has passed away,
We will spend eternity praising His name.
Our hearts will be united in glory,
Never to feel sorrow again.

Forgiveness

Will your eyes fill with tears
When you hear that I am gone?
Or, will your heart be lighter,
Knowing that my life is done?

I tried to make amends with you;
I guess it was in vain.
I'm so sorry that I hurt you.
I never meant to cause you any pain.

My life has taken a different turn;
I now see sunshine instead of rain.
His love has changed my soul,
And taught me how to love again.

My prayer is that you will know Jesus,
Forgive, and leave the past behind.
Allow the Lord to change your heart,
The same way He changed mine.

From Darkness to Light

I used to walk in darkness,
Always hiding from the light,
Until my Savior showed me,
How to live my life just right.

I used to frolic in the world,
Not knowing what could be.
Dead to sin, my soul was lost;
Then Jesus came and rescued me.

At first, I was ashamed,
Because of all that I had done.
I confessed that Jesus is God's own Son,
And my sins were washed away.

Now I follow Jesus,
And even when I fall,
He guides me out of darkness,
His light gets me through it all.